COVENANT • BIBLE • STUDIES

Biblical Imagery for God

Christina Bucher

faithQuest™ ✦ Brethren Press™

Copyright © 1995 by *faithQuest*. Published by Brethren Press, 1451 Dundee Avenue, Elgin, IL 60120

Brethren Press and *faithQuest* are trademarks of the Church of the Brethren General Board.

Unless otherwise noted, scripture quotations are from the New Revised Standard Version of the Bible, copyrighted 1989 by the National Council of Church of Christ in the USA, Division of Education and Ministry.

Cover photo by Martha Miller

99 98 97 96 95   5 4 3 2 1

Library of Congress Catalog Card Number: 95-77971

Manufactured in the United States of America

Contents

Foreword

The Covenant Bible Study Series was first developed for a denominational program in the Church of the Brethren and the Christian Church (Disciples of Christ). This program, called People of the Covenant, was founded on the concept of relational Bible study and has been adopted by several other denominations and small groups who want to study the Bible in a community rather than alone.

Relational Bible study is marked by certain characteristics, some of which differ from other types of Bible study. For one, it is intended for small groups of people who can meet face-to-face on a regular basis and share frankly with an intimate group.

It is important to remember that relational Bible study is anchored in covenantal history. God covenanted with people in Old Testament history, established a new covenant in Jesus Christ, and covenants with the church today.

Relational Bible study takes seriously a corporate faith. As each person contributes to study, prayer, and work, the group becomes the real body of Christ. Each one's contribution is needed and important. "For just as the body is one and has many members, and all the members of the body, though many, are one body, so it is with Christ. . . . Now you are the body of Christ and individually members of it" (1 Cor. 12:12, 17).

Relational Bible study helps both individuals and the group to claim the promise of the Spirit and the working of the Spirit. As one person testified, "In our commitment to one another and in our sharing, something happened. . . . We were woven together in love by the Master Weaver. It is something that can happen only when two or three or seven are gathered in God's name, and we know the promise of God's presence in our lives."

The symbol for these covenant Bible study groups is the burlap cross. The interwoven threads, the uniqueness of each strand, the unrefined fabric, and the rough texture characterize covenant groups. The people in the groups are unique but interrelated; they are imperfect and unpolished, but loving and supportive.

The shape that these divergent threads create is the cross, the symbol for all Christians of the resurrection and presence with us of Christ our Savior. Like the burlap cross, we are brought together, simple and ordinary, to be sent out again in all directions to be in the world.

For people who choose to use this study in a small group, the following guidelines will help create an atmosphere in which support will grow and faith will deepen.

1. As a small group of learners, we gather around God's word to discern its meaning for today.
2. The words, stories, and admonitions we find in scripture come alive for today, challenging and renewing us.
3. All people are learners and all are leaders.
4. Each person will contribute to the study, sharing the meaning found in the scripture and helping to bring meaning to others.
5. We recognize each other's vulnerability as we share out of our own experience, and in sharing we learn to trust others and to be trustworthy.

Additional suggestions for study and group-building are provided in the "Sharing and Prayer" section. They are intended for use in the hour preceding the Bible study to foster intimacy in the covenant group and relate personal sharing to the Bible study topic.

Welcome to this study. As you search the scriptures, may you also search yourself. May God's voice and guidance and the love and encouragement of brothers and sisters in Christ challenge you to live more fully the abundant life God promises.

Preface

We have joked in our office about "Dishtowel Theater," the way we use dishtowels for headdresses and bathrobes for garb resembling the clothing of ancient Near Easterners in our little church dramas. But when it comes down to it, those silly costumes always pop into my head when I think of Bible characters.

And when someone addresses God in prayer, I can't help but think for a fleeting moment of a person, a man in white robes and a flowing beard. I know in my mind that God is infinitely greater than a man, but as a child I found it easier to picture God as a person than to figure God is love, and now the thought of God as a man will not let me go. I have, in essence, "engraved" an image of God on my mind, just as the Ten Commandments tell us not to do.

I don't think I'm the only one who is so weak as to presume things about God. But there is hope. As Christina Bucher helps us see, there are two solutions to our idolatry. One is to refrain from making any images of God at all. God Is Who God Is, and Was, and Will Be. We can leave it at that. Or we can try to see God in many images, each one giving us a little fuller picture of the indescribable I AM, none being sufficient alone.

This study leaves me knowing less and more at the same time. It properly reminds me that I know less about God than I always think I do. And it introduces me to whole new ways of thinking about God that come directly from scripture. If I don't come away from Bucher's interpretation of the scriptures with a greater understanding of God, then I had better not talk about God at all, either out of reverence to the unknowable deity or to avoid displaying my ignorance.

Read on and delight in the rich ways we can know the great I AM.

Julie Garber
Editor

Recommended Resources:

Drescher-Lehman, Sandra. *Waters of Reflection.* Good Books, 1993.
McFague, Sallie. *Models of God.* Fortress, 1987.

1

I AM WHO I AM
Exodus 3; 20:4-6

*God chose not to reveal any particular name to Moses. No
human word is sufficient to capture all that God is. While
the Bible is full of beautiful, fearful, and loving imagery
for God, we recognize the limits of language. God is
greater than all these.*

Personal Preparation

1. When someone begins a prayer with "Dear God," what picture immediately comes to your mind?
2. Think of as many words or phrases as you can to finish the sentence "God is like . . . ." Think of as many ways as you can that God is like fire.
4. Be aware this week of the names you use to address God in prayer. Also think about your own first and last names and what they mean.

Understanding

Sometime during my first few weeks at seminary, I got into a discussion with two seniors. I suppose they were trying to figure out my theological orientation. Was I conservative? liberal? When they asked, "What do you think about God?" I stunned them with the response "I don't like to talk about God."

What I meant was—after all I did spend three years at seminary talking quite a lot about God—I feel trapped between the necessary and the idolatrous. By necessary I mean as humans we are limited in our ways of communicating our understanding of God. If we are to talk about God, we must use language and images drawn from human experience. But if God is truly transcendent, then our language falls short of fully describing God. That's not so bad as long as we understand that our God-talk has limits. We have to realize that we can only say something about what God is *like,* without ever fully capturing who God *is.* Too often, however, we forget this, and we begin to think God is actually what we say about God. And that is idolatry.

Images

In the second of the Ten Commandments, God tells us, "You shall not make for yourself an idol, whether in the form of anything that is in heaven above, or that is on the earth beneath, or that is in the water under the earth. You shall not bow down to them or worship them; for I the LORD your God am a jealous God, punishing children for the iniquity of parents, to the third and fourth generation of those who reject me, but showing steadfast love to the thousandth generation of those who love me and keep my commandments" (20:4-6).

This prohibition can be understood in two different ways. When the translation prohibits "worshiping an idol," it suggests that we are prohibited from worshiping anything other than God. For polytheistic cultures, that means no worship of other gods. For monotheistic cultures where people believe in only one god, it is often suggested that the second commandment is warning us not to deify money or status or power (which are often precisely those things deified by the culture).

When the translation prohibits "making images" (REB), it prohibits trying to capture God's essence in a statue or picture. The Israelites lived among peoples who worshiped many gods, and an accepted aspect of their polytheistic worship was the making of images of their gods. Archaeologists have uncovered many of these statues of ancient Near Eastern deities. Some are small images that could be hung around your neck or held in your hand. Other larger images sat inside temples, symbolizing the presence of the deity. Worshipers might bring food to the temple for the deity, and priests might bathe and dress the image as an expression of devotion.

Israelite worship, however, differed from Canaanite, Babylonian, and Phoenician worship in its prohibition of God-images. We know that Israelites observed the prohibition (at least at some point in their history), because archaeologists have failed to dig up statues or other images of the Israelite God. (It may be that some Israelites did make images of their God, but later generations destroyed them.) Why did Israelite worship prohibit the making of images of their God? Perhaps they feared that worshipers would fail to distinguish between the God-image and the God who can be known but not fully comprehended.

Symbolism

Though we often tend to box God in, the idea that God is beyond our full comprehension is at the back of our minds, even for children. My four-year-old son, Zachary, surprises me by initiating conversations about God. One day as we were driving home from preschool, he said, "My friends told me that God is in one place, but I said they were wrong—God is everywhere." On another occasion, I was explaining how we breathe oxygen into our lungs and breathe out carbon dioxide. He looked puzzled, so I said, "Oxygen and carbon dioxide are invisible; we can't see them." Zach grinned and said excitedly, "Oh, so there are three things that are invisible: those two things and God!" How will I help him connect that invisible, omnipresent God with the other images of God in the Bible, images that portray God in human form?

I have always been fascinated by the story of the call of Moses in Exodus 3, but I never could make much sense of it until I began to learn about storytelling in much of the Bible. For many years I read the Bible so seriously, so literally, and I had so many questions about what I read. I talked to my parents, my Sunday School teachers, and pondered the questions in my heart. How could a bush burn but not be consumed? Why choose this way of appearing to Moses, when in other places Moses actually sees God? Why does verse 2 refer to an angel in the bush, but verse 4 says God called to Moses from the bush?

As I got older and came to understand symbol, I began to understand this passage. Fire cooks our food, warms our bodies, enables us to see in the darkness, and, so, is essential to our lives, just like God. Nevertheless, we must treat fire carefully, for it can also destroy, just like God. I began to see that in the Bible God frequently appears to humans in fiery form and that fire in the Bible commonly symbolizes holiness. Both can purge and purify, and both can destroy.

The bush that burns but is not consumed attracts Moses' attention. He is drawn to it, fascinated, yet fearful. How can this be? He wants to know more, but as he approaches—as God surely intended him to—he is warned. This is holy ground. Take off your shoes.

As Moses discovers, seeing God or being in God's presence is never sufficient in and of itself. It leads to some action—in this case the call of Moses. And the action is always connected to our world. "You've seen me, Moses, now carry out my instructions. Go, rescue your people." God acts in our world, but we are the actors who carry out God's mission.

Moses is less than thrilled. Only a short while ago he had been tending his flock, minding his business, and now he's supposed to go back to Egypt to challenge the power of Pharaoh. Who among the Israelites will believe him? What authority does he have to carry out God's plan for Israel's liberation?

Moses comes up with a ploy. He asks this divine being to reveal his name. If the god refuses, Moses is off the hook. If the god reveals his name, Moses has gained power, since knowing someone's name gives you power over them. Just as Jacob had asked the name of his mysterious wrestling partner at the Jabbok, so Moses asks the name of this mysterious presence on the mountain.

Names

Names have power. Our names tell something about us but they also have a way of requiring that we live up to them. Parents pore over books of baby names in search of just the right name for their unborn child, a name that will capture the child's personality and help form its character. Name changes signify life changes. Children abandon childhood diminutives in favor of their full given names as a sign of their move into adulthood. At marriage a wife may replace her family name with her husband's family name to symbolize her change in status. Some couples choose to symbolize the new entity formed through their marriage by combining their family names. In the Bible, name changes symbolize major life changes for Abram, Sarai, Jacob, Ben-oni, and others. If Moses can know this god's name, he will know with whom he is dealing and be on a more level playing field as they jockey for position.

In response to Moses' question about the divine name, God cleverly replies, "I AM WHO I AM." Some people see in this response a statement of God's unchanging, timeless being. But the Hebrew language has no way of expressing precisely that idea because it lacks a present tense. The Hebrew verb-forms here express incomplete action, not essential being. Another possible translation of the sentence is "I will be who I will be," pointing more to the freedom of God than to the unchangeable nature of God.

Rather than struggling to achieve a precise understanding of this phrase, some people believe God's response is purposely evasive. God refuses to give Moses the divine name, thereby denying Moses power over the deity. "What's your name?" Moses asks, and he is told, "I'm beyond naming and names. I'm beyond your control. I'm beyond your full comprehension." If God were to reveal to us the full-ness of the divine self, who could bear it? God is God and not human. We are humans and not God.

As humans, we are caught between necessity and idolatry. We need our words and images if we are to talk with each other about God. But when talking about God, let us proceed with caution, removing our shoes, lest we succeed only in creating a god who is no God at all.

Discussion and Action.

1. Names have power. Do you prohibit some people or companies from knowing your name (for example, credit card companies or organizations seeking funds)? How do you answer the telephone? Do you give the person on the other end your name or do you just say hello? How does controlling your name give you power?

2. Offer some of the sentence finishers you thought of for the preparation questions. As responses are compiled, do you get a fuller picture of God? What is missing from the list?

3. Make a bookmark for your Bible by writing on a strip of paper various forms of address for God that avoid using a name, such as Blessed One, or I AM WHO I AM. Place between two slightly larger pieces of clear, self-adhering shelf paper.

4. Do you enjoy talking about God or do you avoid talking about God? Why? How do you pray to God? Do you always use the same form of address, or do you use various forms? Why?

5. Are there images of God in the Bible that you avoid? What are they? Why do you avoid them?

6. Close by singing "Immortal, Invisible, God Only Wise."

2

Sovereign God
Psalms 23 and 47; Mark 1:14-15; Luke 17:21

*The image of God as king, drawn from the political world,
serves to emphasize not only God's power, but also God's
care and concern for us as subjects in the divine kingdom.
Jesus' message about the kingdom of God builds upon the
metaphor of God as King to help us understand what it
means to live according to God's will.*

Personal Preparation

1. Close your eyes and try to picture a king in your mind's eye.
   What image comes into view? What does the king look like?
   What is he wearing? Where is he located—indoors or out-
   doors? If there are other people in the picture, where are they
   located in relation to the king?
2. Read Psalms 23 and 47. What characteristics of God are
   described in these two psalms? Write your own psalm,
   beginning it with either "The LORD is my shepherd . . ." or
   "Clap your hands, all you peoples; shout to God with loud
   songs of joy."
3. Read Mark 1:14-15 and Luke 17:21. What does it mean to
   you when the Bible talks about the kingdom of God. Finish
   the sentence "The kingdom of God is like . . . ."

Understanding

What images come into your mind when you think of a king? Do you
see Arthur and the Knights of the Round Table? a king from a fairy
tale or a nursery rhyme? "Good King Wenceslas" of the Christmas
carol? Such legendary kings appear surrounded by pomp and

pageantry. They sit center stage on their thrones with queens by their sides and knights, lords, and ladies in attendance.

What adjectives do you associate with the word *king*? I think first of "powerful." When I look up *king* in my dictionary, I see that he is "a male sovereign exercising ultimate political authority over a nation-state." Kings are very powerful people.

Power itself is neutral. Kings can use power for good or evil purposes. Good kings use power to provide security for those they rule. Bad kings use power to subjugate and oppress their people. In First Samuel, the Israelites ask their leaders for a king because they need someone to protect them from their enemies (8:5, 19-20). The books of Samuel and Kings chronicle the history of the Israelites, who eventually got their kings. But, as we know, they were ruled by both good and bad kings. Some protected them and some did not. Kings can serve to protect their subjects, but, as the prophet-judge Samuel warns, they can also exploit those they rule (1 Sam. 8:11-18).

Because the ancient Israelites lived for approximately four centuries under the rule of their own kings, the image of God as a king was a very meaningful metaphor. We see it in the Bible not only in the portrayal of God as King, but also in the imagery of the kingdom of God and in the Christian understanding of Jesus as Messiah. The word *messiah,* means "anointed one" and refers to Israelite kings who were anointed when they began their rule. Although Israelites suffered under many human kings who were corrupted by the power they wielded, they conceived of God as the ideal monarch.

God Is King of All the Earth

Psalm 47 praises God as the King who rules over all nations. Other psalms, often referred to as the "Enthronement Psalms" (93; 95—99), praise God who rules over all creation and as one who judges the earth. Although Psalm 46 does not call God "King," it does praise God for protecting us: "God is our refuge and strength, a very present help in trouble" (v. 1).

Psalm 72 describes, at least in part, what the ideal human king should do and, therefore, what God as king does. The king establishes and maintains "justice and righteousness" in the kingdom. Ancient Israelite justice attended to the needs of individuals. Consequently, doing what is right (which is what righteousness is) means offering help to those in need—the weak, the poor, the widows, and the fatherless.

The psalmist expresses the hope that his King, in whose reign peace abounds, will live long (vv. 5-7) and that his rule will extend far and wide (vv. 8-11). A king whose rule is characterized by justice, right-eousness, and peace carries out God's promise to Abraham that "in you all the families of the earth shall be blessed" (v. 17; see Gen. 12:3).

The King as Shepherd

Who doesn't love Psalm 23? The Shepherd Psalm is one of the pas-sages I memorized as a child and can still quote in the King James Version. Psalm 23 is called a "song of trust," and, indeed, this psalm's six lines have the power to create an atmosphere of trust and confi-dence in God that is almost unparalleled.

As far back as the ancient Mesopotamian civilization of Sumer (approximately 3300—1750 B.C.), people referred to their kings as "shepherds." Like a shepherd, a king must care for his flock, keeping them healthy and protecting them from harm. The biblical writers also saw their God in this way—both king and shepherd. In the early church, Psalm 23 was sung at baptism. Today, it is often read at funer-als because of the understanding that God accompanies us through "the darkest valley."

Not only do we think of political leaders as shepherds, we also think of our spiritual leaders as shepherds. For instance, bishops in the Catholic Church still carry a shepherd's staff in worship to signify that they are leaders and guardians of the people.

In a seminary commencement address entitled "Flockfood," church historian Don Durnbaugh gave many soon-to-be spiritual leaders another responsibility as shepherds. Like shepherds, Don observed, pastors have the responsibility of feeding the flock. Pastors feed their flock with teachings through the sermon, which ought to be meaty and substantive. "When Jesus said, 'Feed my sheep,' he did not say harangue them, or put them to sleep, or tickle their ears, or condemn them." Following the example of Jesus, the true Shepherd, the shep-herd pastor's role is to nourish the congregation.

The Kingly Rule of God

We have never been able to define precisely what Jesus meant when he proclaimed the coming of the "kingdom of God." Some describe it as a place. Others call it a way of life. Some think it is present now. Others believe it is beyond this world. And what is a kingdom? Few of us today know what it is to live under the rule of a king. Yet ver-sions of the Bible, such as the Contemporary English Version and *The Message* that try to translate New Testament Greek into everyday English, use the expression "kingdom of God."

I have found in teaching college students that many of them equate the kingdom of God with heaven and assume that entering God's kingdom means going to heaven when they die. The Greek expression commonly translated "kingdom of God," however, refers not to a specific place or time, but to the reality and experience of God's authority. To enter the kingdom, we have only to accept God's rule in our lives. This willingness to acknowledge God's authority enables us to live near God and to experience the justice, peace, and joy that such closeness brings. As a way of making this understanding more clear, some Bible translators propose terms such as "God's Kingly Rule," "God's Realm," and "The Commonwealth of God."

In the Gospels, Jesus announces that the kingdom is both present and near. Which is it, we wonder. Is the kingdom here now, or is it something we anticipate? Or is it both? I have found theologian Dorothee Soelle's explanation of the tension between the "already-ness" and the "not yetness" of God's realm helpful. In her book *Thinking About God,* she suggests that God's realm is more like a relationship to be entered into than an object to be possessed. A relationship in the present always has an openness to the future. If we presume that we know everything there is to know about a friend, we will have destroyed the relationship. Similarly, we enter into God's realm in the present, knowing that there is more to be experienced of that realm in the future (139).

As I think about Sovereign God, I recognize and affirm God's power, but I know that power is not the only attribute—perhaps not even the main attribute—of God as King. The ancient Israelites understood God as King to be powerful, but just as important, the King was the one who showed concern for the very least of his subjects. Israel's Sovereign God is the Shepherd who cares for the flock. Picking up on this imagery, Jesus talked about God by telling the story of the shepherd who went out looking for the one lost sheep out of a flock of one hundred.

As I think about the kingdom of God, I recognize that by choosing to enter into a way of life that acknowledges God's rule, I become a part of a community of people who agree that God's way of doing things is just right.

Discussion and Action

1. Share your images of a king. Talk about your reactions to the image of God as King.

2.   Invite group members to share the psalms they wrote in preparation for this session.

3.   Brainstorm together to come up with additional names for what the Bible calls the "kingdom of God." Can you think of terms that will make this expression more meaningful for people today?

4.   In *Thinking of God,* Dorothee Soelle writes, "Jesus proclaimed the kingdom of God. And what came? What became of it? Disappointingly enough, the church." What do you think she means? Do you agree with her? disagree? In what ways does your congregation show that you have entered the realm where God rules?

5.   In his translation of the New Testament called *The Message,* Eugene Peterson renders the Lord's Prayer as it is found in Matthew in a new way. Read his version together, reflecting silently on his interpretation of the prayer.

Our Father in heaven,
Reveal who you are.
Set the world right;
Do what's best—
          as above, so below.
Keep us alive with three square meals.
Keep us forgiven with you and forgiving others.
Keep us safe from ourselves and the Devil.
You're in charge!
You can do anything you want!
You're ablaze in beauty!
          Yes. Yes. Yes.

3

Judge God
Isaiah 5:1-7; John 15:1-17

*As ruler of the universe, God establishes justice in our world
and judges us against it. In the Bible, writers use garden
images to demonstrate God's justice and how God judges.*

Personal Preparation

1. If you have had any experience gardening, reflect on that
   experience. How did you feel when a fruit tree you had
   planted did not bear fruit? What did you do with the plants
   that failed to yield vegetables? Read Isaiah 5:1-7. Compare
   your gardening experience with that of the vineyard owner.

2. Look up Isaiah 5:1-7 in the King James Version of the Bible
   and compare verse 7 with another translation, such as the
   New Revised Standard Version or the New International
   Version. How do you react to the word *judgment* (KJV)?
   How do you react to the word *justice* (NRSV or NIV)?
   Describe your reactions to these two words.

3. Read John 15:1-17. Draw a picture of a vineyard and its
   grower as described in John. Identify God, Christ, and
   Christ's followers in your picture. Looking at what you've
   drawn, describe the relationships between God and Christ
   and between Christ and his followers that John is talking
   about in this chapter. Plan to take your drawing with you to
   your covenant group.

Understanding

How I envy gardeners. I listen with admiration as my friend Louis
talks about fruit trees he has planted and new varieties of lettuce,

tomatoes, and carrots he is trying out. I shake my head in amazement when I look at the mounds of vegetables Louis produces in his small, raised vegetable bed. I have always wanted to grow a garden, and I've tried several times, but I seem to lack the proverbial green thumb.

I can really identify with the gardener in the prophet Isaiah's parable. He seems to have trouble with his garden, too. The eighth-century prophet Isaiah tells this story of the vineyardist, who represents God, and the wild vines, which are the unfaithful people of Judah and Jerusalem. He uses the thinly disguised parable to seduce the people into listening to what turns out to be a pronouncement of judgment upon them. Isaiah begins the story innocently enough:

Let me sing for my beloved
    my love-song concerning his vineyard:
My beloved had a vineyard on a very fertile hill.

Then Isaiah describes how the vineyard owner carefully prepared the field in order to harvest a good crop of grapes. But when the season is over, the vineyard has produced worthless, sour grapes (Isa. 5:1-2).

Then the prophet's unnamed friend (who is actually God) speaks directly to the people:

And now, inhabitants of Jerusalem and people of Judah,
    judge between me and my vineyard.
What more was there to do for my vineyard
    that I have not done in it?
When I expected it to yield grapes, why did it yield wild grapes?

And now I will tell you what I will do to my vineyard.
I will remove its hedge, and it shall be devoured;
I will break down its wall, and it shall be trampled down;
I will make it a waste; it shall not be pruned or hoed
    and it shall be overgrown with briers and thorns;
I will also command the clouds that they rain no rain upon it. (5:3-6)

Anyone who has gardened will likely identify with the frustration of this vineyard owner. After giving time and effort, after buying fertilizer and mulch, you expect your garden to produce tender sweet corn, moist lima beans, and crisp carrots. If it doesn't, what more can you do?

With the announcement that the vineyardist will withhold the rain (v. 6c), the listeners become suspicious about the identity of Isaiah's as-yet-unnamed friend. Who can command the clouds not to rain? In verse 7, Isaiah reveals to us the identity of both the vineyard owner and the vineyard. They are none other than Yahweh of Hosts and the Israelites. (After the destruction of the northern kingdom of Israel in the eighth century B.C., the southern kingdom—known officially as Judah—took over the broader term Israel for itself.)

> We learn the reason for God's anger.
> He expected justice,
> > but saw bloodshed;
> righteousness,
> > but heard a cry! (5:7b)

The Hebrew version of this statement makes the point simply and dramatically by means of wordplay: God expected *mishpat,* but saw instead *mispach.* He looked for *tsedaqah,* but instead heard a *tse`aqah.* What exactly does this mean? Today's English Version helpfully translates the meaning of the Hebrew text as follows:

> He expected them to do what was good [*mishpat*],
> but instead they committed murder [*mispach*].
> He expected them to do what was right [*tsedaqah*],
> but their victims cried out for justice [*tse`aqah*]. (TEV)

The Hebrew word *mishpat* can be translated either "justice" or "judgment." Biblical justice focuses on people's needs. It attends to the homeless, the poor, those persons oppressed by an unjust political system. In doing so, the homeless, poor, and oppressed are raised up; their oppressors are judged.

At the beginning of this passage, I identified with the frustrated gardener, feeling angry at the vineyard that didn't produce. After finishing the parable, however, I found that I identified with the failed vineyard. How many times have I failed to produce good grapes? When has my community yielded sour grapes? Even though I am not the disappointed gardener, I can understand his frustration with a crop that fails. Knowing that kind of disappointment, I am forced to think about my own part and my community's part in disappointing God. This is Isaiah's intent in telling the story.

The Vineyard in the New Testament

In the New Testament, Jesus also uses the imagery of the vineyard in his parables (see, for example, Matt. 20:1-16, the parable of the Laborers in the Vineyard). In John 15, Jesus, like Isaiah, portrays God as a vineyardist. Here, the image represents the unity of Christ (the vine) and the disciples (the branches). Christ both commands his disciples to be productive (v. 16) and enables them to do so (vv. 4-5).

In this image, God the Vineyardist prunes the branches so that they will produce more fruit (v. 2). Many plants will flourish and thrive better if they are cut back from time to time. The Greek word used here means both "pruning" and "cleansing." Just as grapevines are pruned, disciples are cleansed—in order to make them both more productive. Branches that fail to produce grapes are removed (vv. 2, 6).

Some Christians are comfortable with the image of God as judge. Others are not. We all probably have different images of a judge and different associations with the idea of judgment. What is it about the imagery of judgment that brings discomfort? Is it Jesus' command to refrain from judging lest we be judged ourselves? Is it our image of Judgment Day when everyone learns whether they are in or out of the divine plan? Should we discard the imagery of God as judge?

Think about it. We ourselves make judgments every day. We determine when a bush or tree needs pruning. We decide to pull plants out of our garden if they are not producing. At our jobs, we evaluate the workers we supervise, often deciding who get raises and who don't. Parents are continually making judgments. Imagine what would happen if parents refused to discipline their children. How would those young people develop into moral, responsible adults?

Although discipline and punishment are closely related terms, discipline focuses more on instruction and training, on methods used to develop character in children. Punishment, on the other hand, refers to the penalty imposed upon someone who has done wrong. Parents today are encouraged by child development experts to think of ways to discipline rather than punish their children.

Judgment is a necessary aspect of our lives. The Bible tells us that we are like a garden planted by a God who watches and tends us, hoping for a good crop. When God tends us with loving discipline, our branches will produce.

Discussion and Action

1. Talk about your experiences as gardeners. If anyone has had experience pruning a fruit tree or grapevine, describe how it is done. Now think about the imagery of pruning in John's Gospel. How and when have you experienced "pruning/cleansing"?

2. Close your eyes for several minutes and try to picture a judge. What images come to mind? Are you influenced by television or movie portrayals of judges? Do you have a friend or family member who is a judge? The covenant group may want to invite a judge to talk to the group.

3. Read aloud the paragraph in the Understanding section that defines and describes biblical justice. Do you think of justice as focusing on people's needs? Talk about your understandings of the relationship of judgment and justice. Also, look at your community. Who are the oppressed? Who are the oppressors? What has the church done to bring justice to the oppressed? What more can it do?

4. As a parent, or a child, what kind of judgment works best for you—judgment that punishes or judgment that disciplines?

5. Share your drawing of the vineyard and vineyardist. Talk about your understandings of the God-Christ and Christ-Disciples relationships in John 15:1-17. Read or sing together the hymn "Thou True Vine, that Heals."

4

Creator God
Genesis 1—3; Isaiah 42:5-9;
2 Corinthians 5:17

In the beginning, God created a good world. Since that time, God has continued to create. Even now, God can do new things for the world.

Personal Preparation

1. What words or images do you associate with God the Creator? What feelings emerge when you think of God as Creator?
2. Read the first three chapters of Genesis. How does this account emphasize that what God created was good? What went wrong with the world God created? Is the world as we now know it God's good creation?
3. Read Isaiah 42:5-9 and 2 Corinthians 5:17. Make a list of new things that God has done since the creation of the world.

Understanding

When I lived in southern California, I loved to go camping in the mountains. Sometimes we went up into the nearby San Jacintos. If we had more time, we drove north to the Sierras. I always experienced a sense of peace and well-being there and returned to the hustle and bustle of my everyday life feeling more hopeful.

I know that I am not alone when I describe my feelings about the mountains. There are many who go to the mountains, or the desert, or the seashore for spiritual renewal or recreation. We do it because it makes us feel closer to God.

We can know God in many different ways. We can understand who God is by reading about God in the scriptures. We learn about God as we listen to the Sunday morning sermon. But we also come to know God by looking at what God has created. As I look across the pon derosa pines, as I smell the fragrant hemlock, as I feel the warmth of the sun and hear the crows cawing overhead, I believe that God is love. Who else but a loving God could have created such a world of beauty?

We learn from scripture that God did in fact create a good world. At the end of each of the first five days of creation, we read that "God saw that is was good." And at the end of the sixth day of creation we read that "God saw everything that he had made, and indeed, it was very good" (1:31a). Some creation stories in other traditions claim that the created world is evil, that is was a mistake, or that it was created by an evil deity. In contrast, the Genesis 1 account of creation emphasizes the world's goodness. This understanding is reflected in the rest of the Bible.

What's Wrong?

Into my reverie breaks the evening news. The war continues in Bosnia; the famine continues in the Sudan. Hurricanes and typhoons destroy people's homes. A train derails. Where is the good creation I read about in Genesis? If God created everything good—what has gone wrong?

Over the years Christians have come up with many different ways of answering this question. Some will simply say that it is a mystery that we must accept, but one we cannot understand. This satisfies some Christians, but others feel it important to explore possible ways of increasing their understanding.

Of course, we know from Genesis 3 that our first parents disobeyed God, thereby destroying the relationship that existed between them and God, between them and the rest of creation, and between each other. But why did God create humans, knowing they would disobey? Looking at the havoc brought about by humans over the centuries, some Christians ask, "Was it worth it?" Why didn't God create automatons or robots who would obey? Instead, it seems as if God purposely made creatures who would choose to bring sin and death into the world.

In response, some blame the devil (or Satan). They say that God created a good world and good human beings, but that the devil tempts them to do wrong (even though in Genesis 3 it was not the devil, but an animal created by God, that tempted Eve). This may seem to take the blame off God, but if we think about it very long, we have to ask, Where did the devil come from? If God created everything, God must have created the devil, too!

If God created evil as well as goodness, does that mean God is more vengeful than loving? Some Christians would say that God is certainly not all-loving. They point to examples in scripture of what seems like divine capriciousness. Someone touches the ark of the covenant and is struck dead. Ananias and Sapphira fall down dead when it is revealed that they did not put all of their money in common. While there are indeed some stories of God's vengefulness, most Christians would agree that by nature God always acts with love.

Some Christians say that we have evil in the world because God is not all-powerful and cannot keep evil from happening. Other Christians insist that God is both all-loving and all-powerful and that at some time in the future God will defeat evil and end the suffering of innocent people. According to some, sinners will be punished. Others emphasize the love of God to such an extreme that they believe that ultimately God will bring about the salvation of all creation.

I don't know the answer to this. I do know that sometimes I am more able to accept the reality of evil in the world as a mystery. At other times, when I see pictures of starving children in the Sudan or hear that a friend's daughter has been diagnosed with leukemia, the ugliness of our world threatens to overcome my confidence in a loving and powerful God.

Hope

At these times I find I need to open myself to all of Scripture, to learn not only that God created the earth and everything in it, but also that God continues to create. In the Book of Isaiah, the prophet testifies that God did not finish with creation in six days. God continues to create, so in the moments of our deepest despair we can experience hope that good will come of evil, that evil will not have the last word in creation.

It seems almost impossible to believe that some people will be able to see good in evil. How does the parent who accidentally takes the life of his or her own child, or the Holocaust survivor, or enslaved people in other parts of the world, or people tortured by tyrants see good in the suffering they have endured? To see that hope is possible in such cases, we can look in the Bible at the story of the children of God as they were driven off their land, marched into exile, and stripped of their political autonomy. Israel wept when they remembered Zion.

To this completely demoralized group, the prophet Isaiah announced that God was doing a new thing. I wonder how people responded to this prophet of the Exile. I imagine some thought the prophet crazy; others may have hoped the message was true, but have been afraid to hope too much for fear of disappointment.

Theologian Dorothee Soelle writes, "The important thing is to love creation, to train oneself and one's children to be aware of creation. With my small two-year-old grandson I have planted bulbs in the earth; I have explained to him that now winter is coming and first the flowers have to sleep, and also that the earthworms now no longer come far enough up for us to be able to see them."

From the ugly bulb comes the beautiful flower. Out of chaos came order in the creation. Out of pain, God creates new life and new faith. "Weeping may linger for the night, but joy comes with the morning" (Ps. 30:5).

Discussion and Action

1. Where do you see goodness in God's creation? Describe how goodness makes you feel.
2. Read the quotation from Dorothee Soelle in the Understanding section. Brainstorm ways that you can teach children in your family, congregation, or community to be aware of creation.
3. How would you explain what went wrong with our world? Do any of the views identified in the lesson fit your perspectives?
4. As individuals or as a covenant group, renew a past commitment or make a new commitment to work to care for God's creation.
5. In light of the harsh realities of life, how do you continue to believe that God's creation is good? Tell stories of good things that have come out of chaos in your life or in the world.
6. Talk about how you respond to the idea that God continues to create. Tell about ways God has been doing a new thing in your life.

5

Parent God
Exodus 4:22; Isaiah 49:14-21;
Luke 13:34; 15:11-32

The Bible says that God is a father to us—and God is like a mother. God is like a parent who tenderly cares for us and fiercely defends us.

Personal Preparation

1. Is the idea that God is your parent meaningful to you? Why or why not?
2. Reflect on the image of God as Father. Think about how the Father God image makes you feel. Describe your feelings.
3. A fourteenth-century Christian known as Julian of Norwich wrote, "God almighty is our loving Father, and God all wisdom is our loving Mother." Reflect on the image of God as Mother. Are you comfortable with this image? Do you feel different about God our Mother than you do about God our Father?

Understanding

My son Zachary has a show-and-tell day each week at his preschool. One Tuesday morning as we were getting ready to leave the house, Zach asked if he could take a toy bugle for show-and-tell that day. Because that week's theme was "dinosaurs," I tried to talk him into taking one of his model dinosaurs or one of his dinosaur books. No, he wanted to take the bugle. Again I tried to talk him out of the bugle, thinking to myself that it was a silly show-and-tell, a baby's toy. Zach stood firm, and when I foolishly tried to push the dinosaur theme a third time, he replied angrily, "Well, then I won't take anything."

Good parenting requires us to recognize the independence of our children. Jesus told a story about this very thing when he told the parable of the Prodigal Son. The willingness of the father to forgive his prodigal son strikes us as remarkable. But even before the father accepts his son with open and forgiving arms, we see something even more remarkable. At the very beginning of the story, the father consents to his son's bold request for his inheritance. Today, as in Bible times, a son does not receive his inheritance until his father's death. As Jesus tells the story, however, the father agrees to give the boy his share early without an argument.

When we try too hard to force "what we know is best" upon our sons and daughters, we are often met with resistance, even rebellion. The good father in Jesus' story recognizes his son's independence and allows him to choose to act—even if his choice is a foolish one.

Let's try rewriting Jesus' parable. Imagine that the father initially refuses his son's request. Only after his son's pleading, does he reluctantly give in.

> Dad: You want your inheritance now? You're not old enough to use it wisely. If I give it to you now, you'll probably squander it.
>
> Son: But Dad, I won't squander the money. I promise. I'll invest it wisely. Please, just give it to me now. If you don't, I'll know it's because you don't trust me.
>
> Dad: Well, okay, son, but don't forget—you may draw on the interest, but don't touch the principal. And, for heaven's sake, don't take a chance with the stock market. It's safer to invest in bonds or CDs, even though the return will be smaller.

How would the rest of the story change if we inserted this dialogue into the middle of verse 12? Decide for yourselves, but my guess is that the son could never have returned to his father. At least he could not have come back with the sense of integrity that he has shown us in the parable. Because the father recognizes his son's independence, the son can return, confessing his mistake.

This parable has many meanings and purposes. For one, it tells us something about what God is like. God is like the father who lets his children make their own mistakes and then takes them back when the children confess that things have gone wrong.

Maternal Images

Some Christians today want to encourage us to enlarge our vocabulary for God to include the image of God as Mother. Some say that the exclusive use of masculine imagery for God is sexist. Others argue that thinking about God as Father can even be harmful if we ask those whose earthly fathers and stepfathers abandoned or abused them. Still others suggest that the exclusion of female imagery for God places limits on God that should not be there, that male images attempt to put God in a box.

What does the Bible have to say about this? It is true that in the Bible God is referred to as Father but never as Mother. Nevertheless, some passages do use maternal imagery to describe how God relates to us.

In the Book of Isaiah, we find mother imagery for God in several places. At one point, the prophet praises God for redeeming the Hebrews, who had been exiled to Babylon for their unfaithfulness. In Isaiah 42:14, God declares that caring for the recalcitrant people of Israel is like a woman bearing the birth pangs of labor. God says, "Now I will cry out like a woman in labor, I will gasp and pant." Like a mother, God is willing to endure pain and suffering to bring about new life.

In another place in Isaiah, Zion complains that God has forgotten her. Yahweh protests, "Can a woman forget her nursing child, or show no compassion for the child of her womb?" (49:15) We all know how much a mother loves her infant. Imagine this—God loves us that much, and more.

Fierce Love

The prophet Hosea is known for the variety of imagery he uses to talk about God. For example, Hosea says that God "roars like a lion" (11:10) and that God will "be like the dew to Israel" (14:5). While in Isaiah we see maternal imagery used to portray God's love for us, we find that Hosea pictures God as an angry she-bear. The defensive animal shows the fierceness of divine parental love.

As did many of the prophets, Hosea criticizes the people for turning away from God. In a terrifying passage, God announces that, in response to the Israelites' abandonment of him,

> I will become like a lion to them,
>   like a leopard I will lurk beside the way.
> I will fall upon them like a bear robbed of her cubs,
>   and will tear open the covering of their heart;

there I will devour them like a lion
as a wild animal will mangle them. (13:7-8)

How can God both offer comfort and threaten to devour us? If we think about God's love as parental love, it is not all that difficult to see how God's love for us can be both tender and fierce. Almost every parent finds him or herself staunchly defending a child against critics and then turning around to demand obedience. Who has not found herself in the position of the mother whose child brings her flowers just as the phone rings. The voice at the other end says, "Your child is picking my flowers. Please make him stop." God takes us back despite our disobedience, but God also expects that we will try to become more faithful.

Like Hosea, Jesus lamented his people's refusal to obey God. "Jerusalem, Jerusalem, the city that kills the prophets and stones those who are sent to it! How often have I desired to gather your children together as a hen gathers her brood under her wings, and you were not willing!" (Luke 13:34).

Children do not always take the right path. Sometimes they refuse the comfort and care offered by their parents. Sometimes they make a downright mess of their lives. Imagine the anguish of a parent who can do nothing but watch as a child acts in self-destructive ways. The mystery of free will is that God, knowing what a mess we can make of our lives, grants us our independence anyway.

In an issue of the magazine *Weavings,* priest and writer Henri Nouwen says:

> The parable of the Prodigal Son is a story that speaks about a love that existed before any rejection was possible and that will still be there after all rejections have taken place. It is the first and everlasting love of a God who is Father as well as Mother. . . . Jesus' whole life and preaching had only one aim: to reveal this inexhaustive, unlimited motherly and fatherly love of his God and to show the way to let that love guide every part of our daily lives.

Today Zachary tells me he wants to take something small for show-and-tell, something that will fit in his shirt pocket. I reply, "What a good idea. What do you have that is small enough to fit in there?" Zach thinks for a moment, then, holding up an old, dirty piece of shoelace, he says, "I know! I'll take this shoelace. It's the piece that broke off when you were tying my shoe the other day." I smile and say, "You're right, that *will* fit in your pocket. Tell me about that piece of shoelace." Zach grins. I pass the test.

Discussion and Action

1. Share your feelings about the images of God the Father and God the Mother.
2. If you are a parent, how do you balance your responsibility to guide your children and the need to allow them their independence? Share experiences.
3. What, if any, are the problems of talking about God as a parent? What characteristics of human parents should not be associated with God?
4. What does it mean to be God's child?
5. Isaiah declares that God will cry out like a woman in labor, gasping and panting. What images or memories does that bring to mind?
6. Would the story of the prodigal son be different if the son negotiated with his mother instead of his father? or if the prodigal was a daughter?
7. As a child of God, how would you rate your own obedience? What would you truly deserve from God for your obedience or lack of it? How has God treated you?
8. Talk about ways God is both a comforter and fierce disciplinarian. Suggest tips for ways we can balance love and discipline as parents, relatives, teachers, and mentors.

6

Husband God

Hosea 2:2-23; Song of Solomon 1:2-3; 8:6-7;
Ephesians 5:21-33

The elements of a good marriage resemble the elements of
a good relationship with God. But even in our unfaithful-
ness, God is like a committed husband who cannot leave us.

Personal Preparation

1. In your mind, complete this sentence: God is like a husband
    because . . . . Then read the Bible passages for this session.
    How do you think the different Bible writers would finish
    this sentence?
2. Think of marriages you know. Which ones most closely
    exemplify the "marriage" of God and the people?
3. Write down your ideal marriage covenant and your ideal
    relationship with God. How are the descriptions alike or dif-
    ferent?

Understanding

"Marriage is a noose," said Miguel de Cervantes, the Spanish author.
But to Martin Luther, "there is no more lovely, friendly and charming
relationship, communion or company than a good marriage."
Whatever we feel about our own marriages, Bible writers found that
marriage was an apt way of talking about our relationship to God.

Marriage is one of the three most often used metaphors in the Bible
to speak of God's relationship with the people. The parent-child
metaphor, which we looked at in session 5, may possibly be the old-
est of the three. Another, the ruler-subject relationship, is used more
frequently than the others and was important in shaping the religious

views of both Judaism and Christianity. But surprisingly, the husband-wife image also appears frequently in the Bible. The first time we see it is in the book of the prophet Hosea.

Hosea 2:2-23

The opening of the Book of Hosea is jarring. God tells Hosea to take an adulteress as a wife and create a family with her. How could the God who from Mount Sinai forbade the people to commit adultery turn right around and recommend it to Hosea?

A friend, who experienced a painful divorce from his wife, commented on this passage: "How better to explain the depth of God's disappointment with us when we go astray than to compare it to a husband's frustration with an unfaithful wife." To him, Hosea condemns all idolatry, male or female. Many people on the other hand, seem shocked by this choice of imagery and ask, "Why must a woman represent the faithlessness of the Israelites? Aren't husbands also guilty of adultery?"

It may be that the metaphor of the faithless wife arose out of Hosea's own experience. But we should be careful not to draw from this imagery more than the prophet intended. Certainly, he does not characterize all wives as adulterous or tending toward faithlessness. Nor does he use the imagery to indict Israelite women. Rather, Hosea uses the image of the faithless wife to confront the Israelite people with their disloyalty toward Yahweh.They were the adulterers and idolaters. They were the unfaithful spouses. God is symbolized by Hosea as the faithful one who remains true to the people no matter how poorly they treat their "husband."

Women in ancient Israel were required to be absolutely monogamous in their relationships. Men, however, were not limited in the same way. We know some men had more than one wife, or more than one sexual partner, at a time. Among the patriarchs, Abraham had sexual relations with Hagar while married to Sarah, and Jacob took two wives and two concubines. Kings also could be polygamous. David had several wives, and the Bible reports that among Solomon's wives were "seven hundred princesses and three hundred concubines" (1 Kings 11:3).

Just as Israelite women were limited to one sexual partner, so the Israelite people were prohibited from worshiping more than one god. When we give as much time to the other gods in our lives, such as money, time, jobs, or possessions, we are committing a sort of religious adultery. And in this sense, men are just as guilty of prostitution as anyone.

Hosea talks about God as a husband in order to describe how God "feels" when the people break their covenant relationship. The marriage does not end in divorce, however, as it might in our modern world. God, the husband, expresses his desire to be reunited with Israel, his wife; and the poem concludes with a vision of the reconciliation of God and people (2:14-15, 19-20).

The Marriage Metaphor in the New Testament

In the New Testament, Jesus takes Yahweh's place as Husband or Bridegroom in passages that focus on weddings and the great banquet. The wedding feast or banquet is a symbol of the end of time and the celebration that the faithful will experience in the age to come.

Two parables speak of the wedding feast. In the parable of the Wedding Banquet, a king gives a wedding bash for his son who is getting married, but none of the invited guests bother to attend (Matt. 22:1-14). In the parable of the Ten Bridesmaids, everyone awaits the return of the Bridegroom, symbolizing the Second Coming of Christ. The parable is a warning of sorts to the people to be ready for the Bridegroom's return (Matt. 25:1-13).

In another passage, Jesus is asked why his disciples don't fast as do the Pharisees and John the Baptist's disciples. Jesus replies, "The wedding guests cannot mourn as long as the bridegroom is with them, can they? The days will come when the bridegroom is taken away from them, and then they will fast" (Matt. 9:15). In John's Gospel, John the Baptist refers to Jesus as the Bridegroom and to himself as the friend of the Bridegroom (3:29).

Though Jesus is called a bridegroom in many passages, the identity of the bride sometimes goes unmentioned. Other passages equate the bride with the church. For instance, take Paul's instruction to families in Ephesians 5. As he is telling husbands and wives what their duties to each other are, he compares their relationship to the relationship of Christ and the church. In this case the marriage partnership emphasizes self-sacrifice, just as Jesus sacrificed himself on the cross for the church (v. 25).

Like Hosea, John symbolizes Rome's idolatry as "whoredom" in Revelation 18—19. And he also builds on the symbolism of the wedding. In his vision of the new heaven and the new earth, the prophet John sees "the holy city, the new Jerusalem, coming down out of heaven from God, prepared as a bride adorned for her husband" (21:2). Verse 9 shows the unusual marriage combination of the City (Jerusalem) and the Lamb (Christ).

Through history Christians have continued to use the terms husband and wife as a way of talking about Christ and church. We speak of the wedding feast, for instance, to which we are invited and which we anticipate. Philipp Nicolai's 1599 hymn "Sleepers Awake" is another example of wedding images in Christian life. Long after the Bible, his hymn alludes to the parable of the Bridesmaids and Revelation's Bridegroom-Lamb and wedding feast.

Song of Songs

Despite all the references to marriage in the Bible, tradition has shied away from speaking about the love of bride and bridegroom. Christian mystics have been the exception, and for them the Song of Songs (also known as the Song of Solomon) has been a key text.

I regularly have students in my introductory Bible class read the Song of Songs over Thanksgiving break. Having just worked our way through some of the prophets and struggled with concepts like justice and righteousness, we are usually ready by Thanksgiving for something lighter. When we meet again after the holiday break, I look forward to hearing their reactions to the book. Inevitably someone says, "But this is love poetry! What's it doing in the Bible?"

Although there are no outright references to God in this collection of love poems, both Jews and Christians have seen a lot of religious symbolism in it. Jews have found this poetry to describe something of the way in which God and Israel love and value each other. Christians have understood the two lovers to represent Christ and the Church or, in the case of many mystics, God (or Christ) and the individual soul.

The seventeenth-century French writer Jeanne Guyon believed that Songs referred to the spiritual union of God and the individual. In her commentary on this book, Madame Guyon writes, "You desire your Bridegroom to set Himself upon your heart. He is the source of your life. . . . Let everything be unto Him."

If we truly believe that God is love and that Christ commands us to love one another, doesn't the marriage and human love imagery reveal something of God to us that we do not find in other metaphors? Perhaps we have avoided this imagery in our prayers and study because of its association with sexuality. But sexuality is not the only measure of a marriage. The male-female bond also desires to be together, is concerned for the other, longs to be forgiven and reconciled. These are characteristics of faith as well. Sallie McFague writes in *Models of God*, "Beyond fear of judgment and punishment for sins, and beyond relief and gratitude for forgiveness, lies loving God for

God's own sake because God is God, attractive, valuable, lovely beyond all knowing, all imagining."

From what we know of human love, we can say that our love for God and God's love for us "is strong as death, passion fierce as the grave" (Song of Songs).

Discussion and Action

1. Share your ideal marriage covenants from the preparation section. Compile the descriptions and create a litany about our "marriage" to God. Say: "God is like a husband who . . . ." [Complete with one of the characteristics of an ideal marriage.] Respond after each characteristic with "We praise you God, the forgiving Husband of an unfaithful world."

2. In your opinion does the image of God as a husband mean the same thing for both men and women? Why or why not?

3. In what ways does the marriage relationship provide us with a different understanding of our relationship with God than does the parent-child imagery? the sovereign-subject imagery?

4. Talk about your feelings on divorce. What should we do when our relationships are not ideal?

5. What, if anything, bothers you about the image of God as lover? What, if anything, intrigues you about this comparison?

6. Paul likens self-sacrificial marriage to the self-sacrificial relationship of Jesus and the church. How can the church be self-sacrificing in its love for Jesus Christ? Pass along your ideas to an outreach committee or the pastor.

7

Responsive God
Genesis 18:16-33; Luke 18:1-8

Does our God, who is all powerful and all knowing, also respond to our petitions? The Bible assures us that God listens to us and responds to our pleas.

Personal Preparation

1. Recall your earliest memories about God. Would you say that God seemed more steadfast, unmovable, and unchanging or more bending and responsive? How have these perceptions changed over the years?
2. Read the texts carefully. What do they say about God? When we say we have a relationship with God, what does that mean? If we respond to God, can God also respond to us?
3. What attributes of God never change? What attributes may change?

Understanding

In my childhood years of Sunday school and church-going, it must have been impressed upon me rather firmly that God does not change, because when I got older and began to read the Bible more seriously and thoroughly, it surprised me, no, it shocked me to read stories in which God appears to change his mind.

Genesis 18 is one of those passages. We see Abraham here negotiating with God over the fate of the city of Sodom. Sodom! Not the blessed city of Jerusalem, not Jericho or Bethel, but Sodom, the city that we today associate with total corruption. Perhaps "negotiating" is too nice a word for what Abraham engages in with God. It is really more like haggling, as one might do when buying a car.

When Abraham gets wind of God's plan to destroy Sodom, he approaches God, asking:

> Suppose there are fifty righteous within the city, will you then sweep away the place and not forgive it for the fifty righteous who are in it? Far be it from you to do such a thing, to slay the righteous with the wicked, so that the righteous fare as the wicked! Far be that from you! Shall not the Judge of all the earth do what is just?

> And the LORD said, "If I find at Sodom fifty righteous in the city, I will forgive the whole place for their sake." (Gen. 18:24-26)

Abraham humbly but persistently keeps asking God if he will spare the city if even fewer and fewer righteous people are found. And each time, God says yes, even when Abraham asks if ten are enough to save Sodom.

Does God find ten righteous people and halt the plan to destroy the city? No, but he finds four (Lot and his family) and he rescues them. Biblical scholar Walter Wink concludes that the moral of this story is: It pays to haggle with God.

Persistence Pays Off

Which one of us has not tried bargaining with God? How many times have we as children or adults promised to live a life of devotion and perfection if only God will spare us from everything, from sitting next to the class bully at school to the ravages of a terminal illness? Like Moses we ask for God's help hesitantly because somewhere in the back of our minds, we have the impression that God is unapproachable. On the other hand, we also know God is a loving God who cares for us deeply.

Haggling with God has a long tradition in the Bible. After the construction of the golden calf, Moses intercedes with God on behalf of the Israelites (Exod. 32:7-14). The result of their conversation is that "the Lord changed his mind about the disaster that he planned to bring on his people" (v. 14). In Exodus 33 and Numbers 14, we read again that Moses had to "speak" with God on behalf of the people. The prophet Amos also attempts to intercede with God, but fails (Amos 7—9). And Jonah. That reluctant prophet Jonah was so successful in chastising the Ninevites that after hearing his announcement of judg-

ment against them ("Forty days more and Nineveh shall be over-
thrown"), they repented. And what did God do? "When God saw
what they did, how they turned from their evil ways, God changed his
mind about the calamity that he had said he would bring upon them;
and he did not do it" (Jon. 3:10).

New Testament writers also tell of times when people tried to per-
suade God.

In Luke 18, Jesus tells a parable that has to do with persuasive
prayer. A widow in a city comes repeatedly to a judge to ask for justice against her opponents. The judge, who is described as neither
God-fearing nor people-respecting, refuses her request over and over
again until one day he thinks: "Though I have no fear of God and no
respect for anyone, yet because this widow keeps bothering me, I will
grant her justice, so that she may not wear me out by continually coming" (vv. 4-5).

The moral of the story? Persistence pays. Not only with stubborn
judges, but also with God. For Jesus comments, "And will not God
grant justice to his chosen ones who cry to him day and night?" If persistence pays with an uncaring judge, how much more will it be
rewarded by a caring God.

Why does Abraham haggle with God over the fate of Sodom if he
doesn't believe that God will change his mind? Why does Jesus teach
us that God grants justice to those who "cry to him day and night"?
For that matter, why do we pray to God, petitioning God for changes
in our own lives or interceding with God on behalf of someone else?

Some people say that in petitioning God we change ourselves, not
God. That we become more able to accept what happens to us as a
consequence of praying. That is no doubt true. But it may also be that
our prayer opens a door to new possibilities. Again, in his book called
Engaging the Powers, Walter Wink describes what happens in inter-
cessory prayer this way: "The change in one person thus changes what
God can thereby do in that world."

The character and nature of God does not change. But if we are to
live in a truly dynamic relationship with God, God must be able to
respond to our actions. A man's son asked to borrow his dad's car one
day. Although this father was inclined to refuse the request at first, he
said instead, "Let me think about it, son." When he began to think of
the alternatives, such as borrowing a sports car or driving a friend's
unreliable car, he came to the conclusion that his son would likely be
safer in his parents' vehicle. The father agreed to loan his car. The
father did not change, but with the change in circumstances, the father

could make a different decision. God is like a parent who, although unwilling at first to comply with a child's request, says instead, "Let me think it over."

God relates to us. God feels the effect of both our obedience and sin. We feel the effect of both God's love and judgment. We are fully under the lordship of God, but God hears us and responds. If we must allow God full sovereignty over our lives, then we must also allow God the prerogative to do a new thing.

Discussion and Action

1. Relate your earliest images of God. Tell how your images have changed over the years, if they have.
2. What does it mean to you to be in a relationship with God?
3. From your vantage point as a parent or child, how is God like a parent who hears a child's petition?
4. Are our prayers ever useless? Why or why not?
5. Name hymns, such as "Immortal, Invisible God Only Wise," that picture God as unchanging. Then name hymns, such as "What a Friend We Have in Jesus," that talk about how God responds to us. Recite or sing some of the hymn texts. Talk about which ones are most meaningful to you.
6. How do you react to Abraham's haggling and the woman's persistence before the judge? What keeps you from persevering with God? Or when have you persisted even though it seemed as if God did not hear? What happened?
7. When have you seen God do a new thing?

8

Storm God, Spirit God, Friend God
Exodus 19; John 4:24; 15:13-15

God is as fearful and unapproachable as a storm and as near and familiar as a friend. Saying yes to contrasting views of the Divine, such as these, keeps us from pigeon-holing and trivializing God.

Personal Preparation

1. Of the images of God in this session, choose the one you think of least and address God in this way this week.
2. Which of these two is your favorite? What does it lack?
3. How do you show reverence to important people in your life? How do you show reverence to God?

Understanding

As someone who spends a lot of time thinking, writing, and teaching about God, I worry about becoming too comfortable talking about God. What if I were to lose the sense of God's awesomeness? What if talking about God became matter-of-fact? What if I were to whittle God down to my size?

The Jewish tradition has a way of protecting the awesomeness of God. They avoid pronouncing God's name. The God of the Hebrew Scriptures (the Old Testament) has a name, but we no longer know how to pronounce it the way the ancients did. All that remains are the four consonants YHWH. The Bible was originally written only in consonants, and by the time the Jewish scribes decided to add vowels, they had already begun the practice of using the Hebrew term of respect, *Adonai* (which means "Lord") instead, whenever they came to the Hebrew name for God, YHWH.

Many Jews continue the practice of avoiding direct reference to the deity as a way of showing respect. Some say *hu-Shem*, "the name." In Jewish writing, you may see "G_d," again as a sign of reverence. Other forms of address such as "the Holy One, Blessed be He," are also used. In the New Testament, Matthew avoided being too familiar or informal by using the term "kingdom of heaven" where the other Gospels say "kingdom of God."

One way I practice reverence for God is to meditate on passages such as Exodus 19. It periodically reminds me how fearsome and awesome God is. The former slaves have escaped the clutches of their oppressive masters and have come to the wilderness of Sinai. After struggling to make it in the forsaken desert, they are less than grateful for having been saved. If you've visited the Sinai Desert or seen photographs of the mountain thought to be the biblical Mount Sinai, you can probably understand why the Israelites grumbled. I can just hear them saying, "You've brought us here, Moses? This makes slavery in Egypt look good."

But here at Mount Sinai, God appears to them not as a friendly, welcoming presence or a comforter, but as an awesome deity to be approached with fear and trembling.

A mountain is the standard place in scripture where people experience the mind-blowing power of God. At Sinai, Moses met God and received God's instructions (Torah) for the people. On Zion, Solomon built a house for God so that God could be present with us on earth. In the Gospels, the site of Jesus' major sermon was on a mountaintop, as were Jesus' temptation, transfiguration, and ascension.

We still treat mountaintops as a place of reverence, a place where we sense the presence of an immense God. In the speech he gave the evening before his assassination, Martin Luther King, Jr., alluded to Mount Nebo, the mountaintop where God permitted Moses to look over into the promised land: "He's allowed me to go up to the mountain. And I've looked over, and I've seen the promised land. I may not get there with you, but I want you to know tonight that we as a people will get to the promised land." Knowing now that his words were prophetic, we get yet another sense of the awesomeness of God.

On the mountaintop at Sinai, God's appearance is described using the terminology of a thunderstorm: "there was thunder and lightning, as well as a thick cloud on the mountain" (Exod. 19:16), and God speaks to Moses "in thunder" (v. 19). Imagine the effect this had on the people huddled below. Ever since I was a child I have feared thunderstorms, but at the same time I was fascinated by them. I had heard stories about people struck by lightning and had learned all the proper safety precautions, but I still wanted to run outside and look at those jagged flashes of light cutting quickly across the heavens. It is possible to fear something and also be drawn to it.

Bible scholar Walter Brueggemann criticizes contemporary religiosity that doesn't respect the fearsomeness of God. He observes that many of us today trivialize both God and mountaintop experiences by making God too immediate, too available, too much under our control. In the New Interpreter's Bible, Brueggemann says, "We drop to our knees or bow our heads and we imagine that God is eagerly awaiting attention."

We need to read and reread these stories of the dangerous God, the God who is unapproachable in the mountains, of the threatening Storm God, in order to remind ourselves not to get too comfortable with our ideas about God. Without this understanding of the awesomeness of God, we do not fully appreciate God's more intimate presence with us through the Spirit and the mystery of God taking human form in Christ.

The Presence of God

By contrast, the Bible also talks about God's presence with us when it speaks of the Spirit of God. God's Spirit was active at creation (Gen. 1:2). It empowers individuals to act and speak for God. It inspired the prophets. And in Acts 2, God's Spirit comes upon the entire church gathered for Pentecost. When the evangelist John says that "God is spirit" (John 4:24), he is talking about the way in which God interacts with us. God gives to us the Spirit that abides with us forever (John 14:16-17).

God as Spirit is far more approachable than the Storm God, more like a friend. Although the Bible never refers directly to God as "Friend," theologian Sallie McFague says that friendship may appropriately describe one aspect of our relationship with God. Just as we choose to be friends with someone, we choose to be in covenant relation with God. Friendship is characterized by joy, just as our relationship with God is a joyous one. Good friends are united by a common vision. God and God's people together seek the well-being of the entire world and, therefore, share a common vision.

Although God is never called "Friend" in the Bible, Abraham is called God's friend (Isa. 41:8; 2 Chron. 20:7; James 2:23), and Exodus reports that God speaks to Moses "as one speaks to a friend" (33:11). And in John's Gospel, Jesus calls the disciples "friends."

> No one has greater love than this, to lay down one's life for one's friends. You are my friends if you do what I command you. I do not call you servants any longer, because the servant does not know what the master is doing; but I have called you friends, because I have made known to you everything that I have heard from my Father. (John 15:13-15)

One problem with the friendship imagery is that it is sometimes interpreted as an exclusive club that is alien to the gospel message. In adolescence, for example, friends often form cliques, which serve to exclude all those who are not like the insiders. Look at Jesus' friendships, however. He befriended "tax collectors and sinners" (Matt. 11:19). Unlike those who seek friendship with their own kind, Jesus extends the hand of friendship to those outside the circle.

Notice how often Jesus eats with outsiders. His table fellowship with outsiders can be seen as a symbol of the messianic banquet and of God's friendship with us. In the Bible the act of eating together signifies closeness, intimacy, and friendship. Perhaps it is because Abraham showed hospitality to the three strangers sent from God that he is termed a "friend of God." A meal, to which Moses, Aaron, Nadab, Abihu, and seventy elders are invited, ratifies the Sinai Covenant (Exod. 24:9-11). The most frequently reported miracle in the Gospels is of Jesus feeding the crowds. Jesus' last supper with his disciples is the beginning of our practice of Communion, which is a precursor to the messianic banquet. In Luke's Gospel, two disciples come to recognize the man they journeyed with on the road to Emmaus only after offering him the hospitality of a meal.

Today we join with God in friendship when we extend the hand of friendship to those outside our normal circle of friends and acquaintances. We become God's friends when we show hospitality to strangers, and when we do, we experience a foretaste of the messianic banquet at which all peoples will sit at table together.

Difficult as it is, we hold together both understandings of God. God is "wholly other," the one to be approached gingerly with our shoes in our hands, in fear and trembling. God is also with us as Spirit and as Friend. If we see only one side of God—God the Friend—we run the risk of trivializing the greatness of God. And if we focus too much on the awesome God, we miss the mystery of God's Spirit surrounding us. In the end we strive to know both divine presence and divine distance.

Discussion and Action

1. Which view of God, the distant or the present, was emphasized more in your religious upbringing? Does this image stay with you today? How has it changed over the years?
2. How do you show respect or reverence for God in your daily life? In what ways have we, like the Hebrews, failed to show respect for God?
3. Name a mountaintop experience in your life when you experienced the awesome presence of God. How did it feel?
4. Examine the practices of your covenant group or congregation. How is God trivialized in these circles? What could your group do to restore reverence?
5. Where does the Spirit of God dwell in your life? When has the Spirit seemed most close? When has it seemed far away?
6. What part do meals play in your covenant or church community? Who takes part in the meals? How can you ensure that meals include everyone, just as in the great banquet in the Bible? Plan to have a meal together. At the meal, talk about how you have been an insider or an outsider.
7. Tell how you have befriended God by befriending someone who is very different from you. What were the difficulties? What were the joys?

9

Warrior God, Peacemaker God
Exodus 15:1-18; Revelation 19:11-21

To declare that God is a God of war as well as a God of peace is not the same thing as declaring that God fights battles for us. The real question is, are we prepared to be on the side of God?

Personal Preparation

1. Read the texts from Exodus and Revelation. How are the images of God like or different from your childhood Sunday school images of God?
2. In what ways would you say God has defended you in your life?
3. Think back over your life. What risks have you taken for God? What sacrifices have you made?

Understanding

Teenage Mutant Ninja Turtles, Power Rangers, James Bond, Dirty Harry, Rambo. All these pop culture characters fit into what theologian Walter Wink calls the "myth of redemptive violence," which pits good guys against bad guys. A struggle ensues between the forces of good and evil, always culminating in the victory of good over evil.

What is wrong with this myth? Wink claims that by watching cartoons or movies or by reading books that embody this combat myth, we escape reality. We enter a fantasy world in which we identify exclusively with the good guys and view the enemies as absolutely evil or demonic. We never see any good in the opponent or any evil in ourselves or our cause. Wink sees the effects of this mythic thinking even at national and international levels, where we set ourselves up as the good guys over against the bad guys (for example, straights against gays, U.S. citizens against immigrants, the West against the East, Christians against Arabs).

Some people, including former President Jimmy Carter, are constantly working against this overly simplistic, self-serving view of things. In a radio interview, Carter was asked about his diplomatic interventions in Haiti and Bosnia. "When you go into mediation sessions," the interviewer asked, "how do you feel sitting across the table from individuals known to have committed human rights violations?" The interviewer's tone belied a disbelief that someone could stoop to meeting with such loathsome people. Carter responded, "Part of the problem is that we in the U.S. tend to see everything and everyone as either good or evil," and he went on to explain how as a mediator he must be able to hear both sides of a conflict.

These observations strike a responsive chord in me. They help me explain why I dislike certain movies and why I don't let my children watch some of the popular TV programs their friends are watching. I am also better able to reflect on some of the biblical texts that I find problematic because of their war imagery.

Should We Avoid Conflict?

"Yahweh is a man of war. Yahweh is his name." These affirmations from Exodus 15 have long troubled me. As someone who thinks of God as a "God of peace" rather than a "Warrior God," I have spent a lot of time trying to understand this image of God in the Bible. If the Warrior God image were limited to one or two passages, it would be one thing. But it's not. The Warrior God and military imagery permeate the Bible—both testaments.

In Exodus God has just rescued the escaping slaves from the hands of the Egyptians. Miraculously, they find themselves free of their former oppressors. In Exodus 14, we read the story of their rescue at the sea. In Exodus 15, we find a hymn praising the God who is responsible for their liberation.

On the one hand, this hymn would seem to be a perfect example of Wink's myth of redemptive violence. Yahweh is pitted against Pharaoh. They struggle. Yahweh emerges victorious.

On the other hand, it is important to think about how we interpret this hymn. With whom do we identify in the hymn? With God? With the Israelites? With Pharaoh and the Egyptians? With whom *should* we identify?

We do know we can't take the role of God because God is power-ful enough to do what we can't do for ourselves. Some readers may identify with the escaping slaves. The Exodus story is popular among victims of oppression, such as the poor in Central and South America, in that it proclaims that God sides with the oppressed against the oppressor. Some readers *should* try on the role of Pharaoh to see if it fits. If it does, the Exodus story speaks a word of warning—God does not support your oppression.

A similar exercise is useful in Revelation. Military imagery appears in full force in the book of Revelation, where Christ takes up the role of warrior. Near the end of John's collection of visions, the seer describes Christ's appearance as a rider on a white horse. This rider "judges and makes war." Recalling the image of the approaching Warrior God in Isaiah 63:1-6, Christ wears a "robe dipped in blood"; he "will tread the winepress of the fury of the wrath of God the Almighty." Riding in front of an angelic army, he confronts his enemy—the beast, the false prophet, and the earthly kings with their armies.

John describes no battle, but rather, simply reports that the beast and false prophet are captured and thrown into the lake of fire. The remaining enemies are killed by the sword. There is no need for a bat-tle, because the real victory has already occurred with Christ's death on the cross, so that the blood that stains this Warrior's robe is his own blood, not that of his enemies.

Does John's Apocalypse exemplify the myth of redemptive vio-lence by encouraging Christians to feel good about themselves because they are on God's side? Some Christians may read the book that way, but if they do, they have not read Revelation carefully. In the letters to seven churches in chapters 2—3, John challenges Christians to engage in self-examination. When have we compromised our beliefs? When have we taken the easy path, avoiding conflict rather than standing up for what we know is right?

Look at Martin Luther King, Jr. He refused to compromise his belief that racism is sin. He went to jail. He went to his death. Catholic Archbishop Oscar Romero challenged the ruling powers in El Salvador to put down their weapons. He was murdered in a church while saying the mass. The nineteenth-century Brethren minister John Kline spoke out against both slavery and military service. He was ambushed and murdered as he was returning to his Virginia home. If we read Revelation carefully, we learn not to assume that God is on our side, but rather to ask ourselves, "Are we on God's side?"

Reckoning with Evil

Does the imagery of God the mighty Warrior authorize our use of violence? Some may say that it does, but I think rather that it forces us
to reckon with the power of evil in our world. I watched the movie
Romero this year with a class of college students. I was surprised by
the number of students who said, "How could this happen? How can
some people torture others? How can they kill those with whom they
disagree? How could anyone murder a priest in a church? We never
knew about this before." I was surprised by my own response. I knew
about the extreme poverty of the Salvadorans. I knew about Romero's
assassination. Yet I was moved to tears, moved to self-examination.
Would I, could I, do what Romero had done—choose God and truth
over my own life?

To those of us who struggle to understand why there is so much
evil in the world, the Warrior God, the rider on the white horse, proclaims in the face of our doubts that God leads the assault against the
enemy. Our prayer should not be "God, be on my side," but it should
be "God, may I be on your side?"

What, then, of peace? Where is God the Peacemaker? The Apostle
Paul refers often to the "God of Peace." Other passages speak of
peace. Corresponding to the prophetic imagery of battle, we find
images of peace, harmony, accord. Isaiah envisions a "peaceable
kingdom," where even the wolf lies down with the lamb (11:6-9) and
speaks of a time when people will "beat their swords into plowshares,
and their spears into pruning hooks" and "study war no more" (2:4).
John envisions a new heaven and a new earth, a renewed creation that
will follow God's defeat of evil.

Wherever battle is waiting to happen—on the Teenage Mutant Ninja
Turtle front or on the killing fields around the world—the Bible demands
that we first examine ourselves to see if we or our cause are perfectly
good. All honest examination will reveal that none of us is entirely good
or entirely evil. Knowing this about ourselves, we finally come to the
realization that our true enemy is evil itself, not people, and it is often
within us, not facing us. More importantly, evil is God's enemy and when
we choose up sides, always ask to be on God's side, the side of peace.

Discussion and Action

1.   The Warrior God and the Peacemaking God are both in the
      Bible. How have you explained to yourself these opposites in
      one God?

2. Tell about a time you think God defended you or something you believed in. Why was God on your side? Tell about the sacrifices you have made or the risks you have taken in order to be on God's side.

3. Take a few moments for self-examination. Write on a card or piece of paper the battles against evil that you need to fight in your own life. As a group talk about ways to combat evil in our midst.

4. Do you avoid reading scriptures about God as a Warrior? Do you avoid reading passages about peacemaking in the Bible? Plan this week to read some of the Bible stories you have avoided. Talk midweek with another member of the group for encouragement.

5. How can we know for sure that we are on God's side?

6. Is it possible to fight evil with evil? What is the consequence?

7. End by singing "Let There Be Peace on Earth" or a familiar song about peace.

10

Suffering God
Hosea 11:1-9; Mark 15:20-39

The God who is greater than our minds can comprehend also suffers more deeply than we can know. In a mysterious way, however, God's suffering is a sign of triumph, a defeat of violence and evil.

Personal Preparation

1. Read Hosea 11 and Mark 15. Remember when you have suffered and try to imagine how much greater is God's suffering.
2. What good things have come from suffering in your life?
3. In our culture we avoid suffering by having many creature comforts, extensive medical care, and entertainment that take our mind off of unpleasantness. This week make a list of ways that you avoid suffering, even at church.

Understanding

God is King, Father, Mother, Shepherd, Warrior, Husband. The transcendent God before whom we stand in awe. The God nearby, who is present with us as Spirit and with whom we share a meal as friends. The Bible portrays God in all these different, yet interrelated, ways, but perhaps the most distinctive image of the Christian God is that of the Crucified God, the Suffering God.

In the New Testament the Suffering God takes human form in Jesus of Nazareth, a man who went to his death rather than compromise his beliefs. In the suffering and death of Jesus, God experienced the pain of all humankind. In Jesus, God truly became Immanuel, "God with us," suffering as we suffer.

In the Old Testament, we also catch glimpses of the Suffering God. The prophet Hosea, for example, compares God's suffering over the people's disobedience to the suffering of parents who grieve because of their children's waywardness.

Hosea 11:1-11

In Hosea 11:1-11, the prophet uses parental, military, and judicial imagery in a unique combination. It begins with a family story that contrasts the loving nurture of a parent and the callous indifference of a child (vv. 1-4). But then this family tale turns into the prosecution's case in a legal complaint against Israel. Initially, the lawsuit is expected to result in Israel's punishment, carried out in the form of military defeat, exile, and enslavement to the military victors (vv. 5-7).

Justice would demand that the Israelites be punished for their failure to uphold their covenant with God. Parental imagery, however, wins out over the imagery of judge and warrior, and parental forgiving love triumphs over the judge's desire to see the guilty punished.

God expresses doubts about the decision to punish Israel (v. 8). The deity has a change of heart (v. 9). In *Harper's Bible Commentary,* Gene M. Tucker says, "Hosea takes human metaphors for God's love as far as they will go and then stresses that the difference between God and human beings involves his capacity for radical, forgiving love." This radical, forgiving love is at the heart of the Christian understanding of the cross.

Mark 15:20-39

In *Thinking About God,* radical love is at the heart of theologian Dorothee Soelle's story about a friend in Argentina who had been arrested, blindfolded, and interrogated for two nights by a group of men she did not know. When the woman stated, "I am a Christian," one of the men laughed and said, "Why are you telling us that? I too am Christian." He then grabbed her hand and placed it on the cross he wore around his neck, as if to prove his identity as Christ's disciple.

For many, the cross has become simply a piece of jewelry, a trinket, an art object, a symbol whose historical origin has been forgotten. The passion story in the Gospels has become so familiar to us, we can read it passionlessly. Try reading it with new eyes. Read it as if for the first time.

Mark refuses to sentimentalize Jesus' suffering and death, but rather, describes it in much of its grim detail. Crucifixion was a barbaric form of punishment that was widely practiced in the ancient world. Victims were stripped naked, flogged, and fixed to an upright stake. A crossbar was sometimes added at the top to form a T.

Death could take days to occur and usually resulted from the cumulative impact of thirst, hunger, exposure, and the effects of the flogging. It was a humiliating, agonizing way to die. The Romans considered it the supreme penalty and used it to punish slaves, political rebels, and those who had committed the most heinous crimes.

In Jesus' case we see a threefold mocking of Jesus by those who pass by (v. 29), by the chief priests and scribes (v. 31), and even by those crucified with him (v. 32). The treatment he receives should convince all who watch that this man does not deserve our respect.

Mark differs from John in including the anguish of the dying Jesus, reminding us of the humanity of this Galilean. Mark's Christ, it seems, truly suffers. Mark, like Matthew, quotes Jesus as uttering a cry of abandonment, "My God, my God, why have you forsaken me?" (v. 34) This sense of absolute despair is less pronounced—some even say absent—in Luke and John. Luke quotes Jesus as saying, "Father, into your hands I commend my spirit" before breathing his last (23:46). In John, Jesus says simply "It is finished," bows his head, and gives up his spirit (19:30).

But Mark presents us with a paradox. Mark's Gospel, like John's, implies that the humbling crucifixion is really the moment of Christ's glorification. What appears to the world as shame and defeat is really honor and victory. This is the One whom we worship, says Mark— this broken, humiliated man who appears to have suffered defeat at the hands of those who hate him. Theologian Walter Wink notes, however, that "the cross marks the failure, not of God, but of violence." Through his death, Christ exposes the evil nature of the worldly powers that enslave and exploit others. Swayed neither to give in to his enemies (who would have let him go if he had confessed) nor to yield to a desire for vengeance against those who sought to kill him, Jesus triumphs. Yet, if we examine the larger context, we see that Jesus makes a royal entry into Jerusalem (Mark 11:1-10) and is anointed as were Israelite kings (Mark 14:3-9).

Christians have thought about the crucifixion in different ways. One view claims that Christ died so that our sins might be forgiven. This view emphasizes the individual's relationship with God and suggests that the demand of an angry God for justice must be satisfied. Stepping in to take our place, Jesus thus atones for our sins.

Others have emphasized a social understanding of Christ's death, viewing it as God's victory over the power of evil to enslave humans to its way of thinking and operating in the world. In this model, we are forgiven for our complicity with the power of evil in the world, but the emphasis is on the change that takes place for us in our world.

The most important thing the Crucified God does for us is that he enables us to resist the claims of those who use violence to dominate others. While living in a forced exile during the tyrannical rule of Idi Amin in Uganda in the '70s, Anglican bishop Festo Kivengere learned that Amin had ordered that the archbishop be killed. Someone asked the bishop what he would do if he found himself sitting with a gun in his hand opposite the dictator Amin. Kivengere replied, "I would hand him the gun and say, 'I think this is your weapon. It is not mine. My weapon is love.' "

The Crucified God calls us to renounce our own desires and to open ourselves to what God wills for us. "For those who want to save their life will lose it, and those who lose their life for my sake, and for the sake of the gospel, will save it" (Mark 8:35). When Oscar Romero was elected archbishop it was thought he would not get involved in politics. He quickly came to identify with the suffering of the poor people of El Salvador, however, and supported their efforts to gain economic reform. Because of his outspokenness, Romero was gunned down while saying Mass in March 1980. Romero's biographer, Jon Sobrino, writes of the martyred priest that "for him, the crucified God became present in the crucified men and women of history. . . . In the faces of the poor and oppressed of his people, he saw the disfigured face of God."

The cross is not the final event. Disciples who participate in Christ's suffering experience the resurrection through their witness to the reign of God, that realm where justice and righteousness triumph over injustice and oppression. Romero received many death threats, but he did not give in to fear. Instead, he promised, "If they kill me, I will rise again in the people of El Salvador." Death has lost its sting.

Discussion and Action

1. Read the scriptures aloud to each other. Then make a list of the ways we avoid suffering in our lives, including avoiding painful scriptures such as these.
2. Recall the kinds of things we say to comfort people who are suffering. Are they helpful? Do they acknowledge the reality of suffering or do they try to erase it? Come up with helpful expressions of sympathy and comfort.

3. Why does God suffer? Why doesn't an all-powerful God eliminate suffering?

4. In your grief, does it help you to know that God suffers, or does the image of a suffering God seem weak to you? Why? In what ways is suffering a triumph? What does Jesus overcome by suffering? What do we as a society or you as an individual overcome by suffering?

5. Plan another time to watch the movie *Romero* together.

6. Look at the table of contents and think about all the images of God you have studied. Has your image of who God is changed?

7. Which images are most meaningful to you? Is there one that encompasses all or one that stands out above the others? Can you say in a nutshell who God is, or do you dislike talking about God at all?

Suggestions for Sharing and Prayer

This material is designed for covenant Bible study groups that spend one hour in sharing and praying together, followed by one hour of Bible study. Some suggestions are offered here to help relate your sharing to your study of *Biblical Imagery for God*. Session-by-session ideas are given first, followed by general resources. Use the ones you find most helpful. Also bring your own ideas for sharing and worshiping together in your covenant group.

Judith Kipp, writer of these sharing and prayer resources, is pastor of Ridgeway Community Church of the Brethren in Harrisburg, Pennsylvania.

1. I AM WHO I AM

☐ Get reacquainted by telling each other your full name, what it means (if you know), its ethnic origins, and how you got it. Don't forget to include name changes or additions due to marriage or adoption. If your group is small, you may want to add nicknames.

☐ Talk about names you use most often for God. Have someone record the list of names for God as people mention them. Keep the list and add to it during each session. What emotions do these names for God reflect for you?

☐ Would you rather color with a box of eight crayons or a box of sixty-four? Think about God as a box of colors. What colors speak to you of God? Tell why.

☐ Look at Isaiah 43:1b and 4a where God speaks these words: "I have called you by name, you are mine. . . . You are precious in my sight, and honored, and I love you." Close with a prayer in which the group says these words to each one in turn. "[name], God says I have called you by name, you are mine . . . You are precious in my sight, and honored, and I love you."

☐ Sing "Asithi:Amen" on page 60. Sing it several more times, substituting other names in place of Lord.

☐ Close by praying the Lord's Prayer together or in pairs.

2. Sovereign God

❑ Sing a hymn about God as King, such as "Come, Thou Almighty King" or "O Worship the King." Take out the list of names for God from the previous session and record the additional names for God that you find in the hymns. You may want to make two columns—one for names, another for adjectives.

❑ Note that in many ways "King" is a title rather than a name. Talk about the titles you have been given in your lifetime (e.g., mister, doctor, grandma, teacher, etc.). How have you stayed the same or changed with each title you acquired?

❑ Many of the images we have of royalty come from fairy tales and fables, most of which we heard in childhood. Try to name a few of them. Is God in any way like these fantasies?

❑ Look for hymns that use the shepherd imagery for God. Read the words as meditation. If yours is a singing group, consider having a hymn-sing of some of the many hymns related to Psalm 23. Here is a partial listing:
 "The King of Love My Shepherd Is"
 "Gentle Shepherd, Come and Lead Us"
 "Savior, Like a Shepherd Lead Us"
 "Thuma Mina"
 "I Am Weak and I Need Thy Strength"
 "The Lord's My Shepherd"
 "My Shepherd Will Supply My Need"
 "He Leadeth Me"

❑ Pray Psalm 23, but try changing every "he" to "you," for example: "O God, you are my shepherd. I shall not want. You make me lie down . . . ."

❑ Remember to change prayer partners if your group has chosen to do so.

3. Judge God

❑ Look for news items on judges, juries, trials, and decisions. Is the God who judges like the courtroom judge? How are they alike or different?

❑ Write a letter to God as Judge. Do you imagine a wise, even-tempered judge who makes articulate, fair judgments? Do you envision a capricious, opinionated autocrat? Is the judge you see something other than either of these descriptions? What "case" are you making to the Judge? Write God's response to you.

❑ Compare hymns such as "Great Is the Lord" and "There's a Wideness in God's Mercy," which refer to God's justice and God's love at the same time. Sing one together.

❑ Add names to your ongoing list of names for God. Say sentence prayers, having each person use a different name to address God.

4. Creator God

❑ Take time to do a meditation together, focusing on God's creation. Each person should sit comfortably and think of a place where they would most like to be. Spend 3-5 minutes in silence noticing the scene, sensing the smells, hearing the sounds, feeling the temperature. Then pray prayers of thanks for God's wonderful creation. Tell each other about your meditation experiences.

❑ A creator is the person who gives life to the creation. Name the person or persons who have given you life literally and figuratively.

❑ Read aloud "To Weavers Everywhere" on page 58. Artists, composers, poets, writers, factory workers, weavers, teachers, quiltmakers, cooks, tailors, and many more are creators. Name five creators and their creations that enrich your life.

❑ Use the words of the hymn "Breathe on Me, Breath of God" (p. 59) as a closing prayer. Have one person read the first stanza aloud, then sing it together; continue to speak and sing all the stanzas of this prayer hymn.

5. Parent God

❑ Read Psalm 131. In her book *Waters of Reflection,* Sandra Drescher-Lehman asks people to read this psalm and "imagine yourself as a tiny baby, being held in the arms of your idea of the perfect mother." Alone or in groups of two or three, write a paraphrase of this text. Then read them to each other.

❑ When Jesus taught his disciples to pray to "Our Father," he radically expanded the way they thought about God. No one had ever addressed God so intimately. No doubt it seemed very strange and uncomfortable to many people. Mention names for God that make you feel uncomfortable. Allow others in the group to illustrate some of these uncomfortable images in stories from their personal experiences.

❑ Becoming a grandmother gave me a whole new set of images of God as parent. Invite a grandmother or grandfather to tell what it's like to be one. Or, reflect on your own grandparents and your relationship to them.

❑ Remember to add to your list of names for God. Spend time writing a prayer to God, using one or several of your "newer" names for God.

❑ Share some of your prayers using different names for God and then close by saying the Lord's Prayer together.

6. Husband God

❑ Is it possible to "fall in love" with God? What does it means to feel passionate about God? If you know a Catholic sister in your community, consider inviting her to meet with the group to share something about her vows and her "marriage" to Christ.

❑ After his resurrection Jesus asks Peter three times, "Do you love me?" Each time that Peter declares his love Jesus instructs him to become a shepherd for his flock. What do you believe you are to do out of your love for God? Encourage each other in these endeavors.

❑ Song of Solomon does not mention God, but some scholars believe it is an allegory describing God's incredible love for us. Think of God's love as you read this passage from Song of Solomon together:

For love is strong as death,
    passion fierce as the grave.
Its flashes are flashes of fire,
    a raging flame.
Many waters cannot quench love,
    neither can floods drown it. (8:6-7)

❑ The song "Praise, I Will Praise You, Lord" says, "Love, I will love you, Lord with all my heart. 0 God, I will tell the wonders of your ways, and glorify your name . . . ." How has your love for God inspired to you to tell others about God? Sing this song if you know it.

7. Responsive God

❑ Draw a time line of your life. Think about all the times you asked God to help you and God responded. Mark these points on your time line. Pair up to talk about the time lines. Did God always respond exactly as you requested, or did God "do a new thing"?

❑ Read Exodus 32:1-10 aloud. Talk about your faith when God seems absent. How do you pray when God seems absent? Use Exodus 32:11-14 to begin prayer. Add your own prayers, asking God to be near and pledging not to abandon God out of impatience.

❑ Make a list of people you know whom you want to hold up to God in prayer. Then in silent and spoken prayers, pray for all people and concerns you have named.

❑ Detecting a responsive God requires a listening people. Spend three to five minutes observing the silence. Close by singing "Spirit of God, Descend Upon My Heart."

8. Storm God, Spirit God, Friend God

❑ People either like storms or are afraid of them. Tell each other experiences you have had with storms. Where do you see God in the storm?

❑ In prayer, picture where you are most often when you sense the presence of the God of Storm. Take turns mentioning these places aloud, pausing between each one to let people imagine the setting you describe and sense God's presence. Then repeat the process, naming and picturing the places you are when you sense the Spirit of God.

❑ Read the words to the song, "My Life Flows On," on page 61, or have someone "line" the song. Reflect on where God is in this song. What part does the storm play here?

❑ Take a few moments to jot down all the qualities of friendship that you can think of. Combine lists on a sheet of newsprint or on a piece of paper. Pray sentence prayers, telling how you have been a friend to God or how you would like to be a friend to God.

❑ Sing "Spirit of the Living God" meditatively. Then think of the Spirit of God as an energizing force in your life. Sing "Spirit of the Living God" again at a quick pace. Sing it through several times. Clap your hands on beats 1 and 3.

9. Warrior God, Peacemaker God

❏ Ted Loder writes in his book of prayers called *Guerrillas of Grace:*

> The notion of guerrillas seems to be rooted in the ancient Judeo-Christian tradition. The Old Testament prophets can easily be conceived of as guerrillas doing battle with the established powers of their day; and their thundering poetic words and images surely can be read as forms of prayer. Certainly Jesus was the pre-eminent guerrilla of grace; he confronted repressive institutions and liberated captive minds and hearts with his words and his life. A prime weapon in his effort was prayer, and it is little wonder that he taught his disciples to pray.

Respond to Loder's comments. If you can obtain a copy of his book, turn to the section of "Prayers of Commitment and Change" and read several of his prayers.

❏ Talk about a time you had to fight for something you believed in. How did you "arm" yourself? What was your source of power? What did you win and what did you lose?

❏ In pairs, come up with a list of opposites that describe the different sides of an issue, such as liberal/ conservative, right/wrong, and religious/secular. Study the list in silence for a while. Then list the traits of God's side, such as grace and justice. Pick a contemporary issue that has been in the news, and talk about how you could be on God's side in that debate.

❏ Pray about the difficulty of choosing God's side and the sacrifices it requires. Close by singing "Jacob's Ladder," with the phrase "soldiers of the cross."

10. Suffering God

❏ The remark "Between grief and nothing I will take grief" is attributed to William Faulkner. Beethoven reportedly said that if he had to choose between the joys and the sorrows, he would keep the sorrows because he learned so much from them. Maya Angelou named a recent book *Wouldn't Take Nothing for My Journey Now.* Share with each other those times when suffering turned into something more.

❑ Save newspapers for a week. As a group, leaf through the pages and clip stories of events that cause God to suffer. Also pick stories of people and events whose actions would be a comfort to God. Sit in a circle and take turns tossing the stories of pain and suffering in the middle. Then place the stories of comfort in the middle. In sentence prayers ask for the wisdom to comfort God.

❑ Read together this affirmation of faith by Alvin Franz Brightbill.

> I believe in God,
>> the giver of grain and bread,
> and in Jesus Christ,
>> the bread of life broken for us,
> and in the Holy Spirit,
>> God's nourishing power in every grain and loaf.
> I believe that Christ is to be leaven in us,
>> so that we may offer the bread of life
>> to the hungers of every human heart.

❑ Remember that the God who suffers is also the God who heals. To close this session, sing "O Healing River" on page 62.

❑ To end this study, review the list of names for God that you have compiled. Are there others you would add? Pray from your list, saying, "We pray in the name of the Father, the Son, the Holy Spirit, [say the other names on your list]." Respond with a choral Amen or Alleluia from your denominational hymnal.

General Sharing and Prayer Resources

Forming a Covenant Group

Covenant Expectations
Covenant-making is significant throughout the biblical story. God made covenants with Noah, Abraham, and Moses. Jeremiah speaks about God making a covenant with the people, "written on the heart." In the New Testament, Jesus is identified as the mediator of the new covenant, and the early believers lived out of covenant relationships. Throughout history people have lived in covenant relationship with God and within community.

Christians today also covenant with God and make commitments with each other. Such covenants help believers to live out their faith.

God's empowerment comes to them as they gather in covenant community to pray and study, share and receive, reflect and act.

People of the Covenant is a program that is anchored in this covenantal history of God's people. It is a network of covenantal relationships. Denominations, districts or regions, congregations, small groups, and individuals all make covenants. Covenant group members commit themselves to the mission statement, seeking to become more:

- biblically informed so they better understand the revelation of God;
- globally aware so they know themselves better connected with all of God's world;
- relationally sensitive to God, self, and others.

The Burlap Cross Symbol
The imperfections of the burlap cross, its rough texture and unrefined fabric, the interweaving of threads, the uniqueness of each strand, are elements which are present within the covenant group. The people in the groups are imperfect, unpolished, interrelated with each other, yet still unique beings.

The shape that this collection of imperfect threads creates is the cross, symbolizing for all Christians the resurrection and presence of Christ our Savior. A covenant group is something akin to this burlap cross. It unites common, ordinary people and sends them out again in all directions to be in the world.

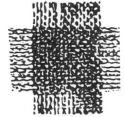

A Litany of Commitment

All:	We are a people of the covenant;
	Out of our commitment to Christ, we seek to become:
Group 1:	more biblically informed
	so we understand better God's revelation;
Group 2:	more globally aware
	so we know ourselves connected with
	all of God's people;
Group 1:	more relationally sensitive to God, self, and others.
All:	We are a people of the covenant;
	We promise:
Group 2:	to seek ways of living out and sharing our faith;
Group 1:	to participate actively in congregational life;

Group 2:   to be open to the leading of the Spirit in our lives.
All: We are a people of the covenant;
            We commit ourselves:
Group 1:   to attend each group meeting, so far as possible;
Group 2:   to prepare through Bible study, prayer, and action;
Group 1:   to share thoughts and feelings, as appropriate;
Group 2:   to encourage each other on our faith journeys.
All: We are a people of the covenant.

The preceding information and Litany of Commitment are from the People of the Covenant program, Church of the Brethren General Board, 1451 Dundee Avenue, Elgin, Illinois 60120.

A Covenant Prayer

O God, we renew the covenant
Spoken by our fathers and mothers,
    sung in homes and meeting houses,
        written by the pens of pilgrims and preachers.
This covenant we know is costly;
    but there is nothing of greater value.
So we accept your gifts and promises
    with thanksgiving;
    And offer you our lives and our love. Amen.

By Leland Wilson. Adapted from *The Gifts We Bring*, Vol. 2 (Worship Resources for Stewardship and Mission).

Through the Week

Consider having a different prayer partner each week. Covenant with each other to get together between sessions, preferably in person, but at least by phone. Partners might discuss their reading and reflection and pray for each other.

Start a collection of imagery for God. On a sheet of paper or newsprint, begin listing names or imagery for God. Add to the list each week. At the end of the study, recite the list, saying "Praise the Lord" after each one.

Look through the Psalms for different ways the psalmist addressed God. Each week, choose one form of address that you do not ordinarily use for God and use it in your prayers for the week. Open each session with prayer, using these more rare forms of address for God.

Most images of God in this study compare God to a human. Leaf through a hymnal to find images of God in animals, objects, or events.

To Weavers Everywhere

God sits weeping,
>   The beautiful creation tapestry
>   She wove with such joy
>   is mutilated, torn into shreds,
>   reduced to rags
>   its beauty fragmented by force.

God sits weeping.
But look!
She is gathering up the shreds
>   to weave something new.

She gathers
>   our shreds of sorrow—
>   the pain, the tears, the frustration
>   caused by cruelty, crushing
>   ignoring, violating, killing.

She gathers
>   the rags of hard work
>   attempts at advocacy
>   initiatives for peace
>   protests against injustice
>   all the seemingly little and weak
>   words and deeds offered
>   sacrificially
>   in hope, in faith, in love.

And look!
She is weaving them all
>   with golden threads of Jubilation
>   into a new tapestry,
>   a creation richer, more beautiful
>   than the old one was!

God sits weaving
    patiently, persistently
    with a smile that
    radiates like a rainbow
    on her tear-streaked face.

And She invites us
    not only to keep offering her the
    shreds and rags of our suffering
    and our work

But even more—
    to take our place beside Her
    at the Jubilee Loom
    and weave with Her
    the Tapestry of the New Creation.

By Marchene Rienstra. From *Women in a Changing World* (June 1987), a publication of the World Council of Churches.

Breathe on Me, Breath of God

Breathe on me, breath of God.
Fill me with life anew,
that I may love what thou dost love,
and do what thou wouldst do.

Breathe on me, breath of God,
until my heart is pure,
until with thee I will one will,
to do and to endure.

Breathe on me, breath of God,
till I am wholly thine,
till all this earthly part of me
glows with thy fire divine.

Breathe on me, breath of God,
so shall I never die,
but live with thee the perfect life
of thine eternity.

By Edwin Hatch, 1878, alt.

Asithi: Amen
(Sing Amen)

Text: South African hymn
Music: S.C. Molefe

My Life Flows On

HOW CAN I KEEP FROM SINGING 87.87 with refrain

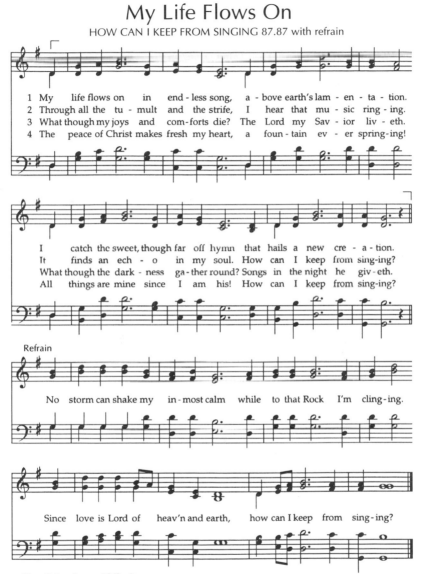

1 My   life flows on   in   end - less song,   a - bove earth's lam - en - ta - tion.
2 Through all the tu - mult   and   the strife,   I   hear that mu - sic ring - ing.
3 What though my joys   and   com - forts die?   The   Lord my Sav - ior liv - eth.
4 The   peace of Christ makes fresh my heart,   a   foun - tain ev - er spring-ing!

I   catch the sweet, though far off hymn   that hails a new   cre - a - tion.
It   finds an ech - o   in my soul. How can I keep from sing-ing?
What though the dark - ness   ga - ther round? Songs in the night he   giv - eth.
All   things are mine since   I   am   his! How can I keep from sing-ing?

Refrain

No   storm can shake my   in - most calm   while   to that Rock   I'm   cling - ing.

Since   love is Lord of   heav'n and earth,   how can I keep   from   sing - ing?

Text: Robert Lowry, 1869, alt.
Music: Robert Lowry, 1869, refrain alt.

O Healing River

Irregular

1 O heal - ing riv - er, send down your
2 This land is parch - ing, this land is
3 Let the seed of free - dom a - wake and

wa - ters, send down your wa - ters
burn - ing, no seed is grow - ing
flour - ish, let the deep roots nour - ish,

up - on this land. O heal - ing
in the bar - ren ground. O heal - ing
let the tall stalks rise. O heal - ing

riv - er, send down your wa - ters, and wash the
riv - er, send down your wa - ters, O heal - ing
riv - er, send down your wa - ters, O heal - ing

blood from off the sand.
riv - er, send your wa - ters down.
riv - er, from out of the skies.

Text: Anonymous
Music: Traditional hymn melody